All About Branches of the U.S. Military

THE UNITED STATES
ARMY

by Tracy Vonder Brink

PEBBLE
a capstone imprint

Pebble Explore is published by Pebble, an imprint of Capstone.
1710 Roe Crest Drive, North Mankato, Minnesota 56003
www.capstonepub.com

Library of Congress Cataloging-in-Publication Data
Names: Vonder Brink, Tracy, author.
Title: The United States Army / by Tracy Vonder Brink.
Description: North Mankato, Minnesota : Pebble, [2021] | Series:
All about branches of the U.S. military | Includes bibliographical
references and index. | Audience: Ages 6-8 | Audience: Grades 2-3 |
Summary: "The Army relies on highly trained soldiers to complete missions
around the world. Learn about the roles of soldiers and their training,
and get an inside look at the advanced equipment, vehicles, and weapons
the Army uses. When duty calls, the Army is always ready to defend"--
Provided by publisher.
Identifiers: LCCN 2020025540 (print) | LCCN 2020025541 (ebook) | ISBN
9781977131737 (library binding) | ISBN 9781977155061 (pdf)
Subjects: LCSH: United States. Army--Juvenile literature.
Classification: LCC UA25 .V79 2021 (print) | LCC UA25 (ebook) | DDC
355.00973--dc23
LC record available at https://lccn.loc.gov/2020025540
LC ebook record available at https://lccn.loc.gov/2020025541

Image Credits
34th Red Bull Infantry Division/Photo by Sgt. Bill Boecker, 25; Army Medicine History/ Photo by Francis Trachta, 13 (Bottom); U.S. Army Flickr for PEO Soldier, 15; U.S. Army National Guard photo by Tammy Muckenfuss, 28; U.S. Army Photo by Staff Sgt. Jennifer Bunn, Cover, 1, 1LT Remington Henderson, 115th Mobile Public Affairs Detachment, 19, Bianka Lathan, 13 (Top), Pfc. Matthew O. Deckelman / 22nd Mobile Public Affairs Detachment, 14, Pfc. Nathaniel Gayle, 22nd Mobile Public Affairs Detachment, 17 (Bottom), Pfc. Steven Young, 27 (Bottom), Pvt. Chantel Green, 11, Sgt. Alex Skripnichuk, 5, Sgt. Dustin D. Biven / 75th Field Artillery Brigade, 17 (Top), Sgt. Gregory T. Summers / 22nd Mobile Public Affairs Detachment, 10, Sgt. Ken Scar, 7, Sgt. Michelle U. Blesam, 23, Sgt. Sarah D. Sangster, 21, Sgt. William Begley/11th Public Affairs Detachment, 27 (Top), Spc. Alex Sensenbach from 1-3ARB, 20, Staff Sgt. Jacob Kohrs, 20th PAD, 24, Staff Sgt. Ryan Sheldon/117th Mobile Public Affairs Detachment (Hawaii), 29, Terrance Bell/ Garrison Fort Lee Public Affairs, 8, Visual Information Specialist Markus Rauchenberger, 9; U.S. Army Reserve photo by Staff Sgt. Austin Berner, 22, Staff Sgt. J Byers, 319th Mobile Public Affairs Detachment, 6, Staff Sgt. Joshua Wooten, 4

Design Elements
Capstone; Shutterstock: CRVL, Zerbor

Editorial Credits
Editor: Carrie Sheely; Designer: Kayla Rossow; Media Researcher: Jo Miller; Production Specialist: Laura Manthe

All internet sites appearing in back matter were available and accurate when this book was sent to press.

Table of Contents

What Is the Army? 4

Joining the Army 6

Army Uniforms and Gear 12

Army Vehicles and Weapons. . . 18

Life in the Army 26

Glossary 30

Read More 31

Internet Sites 31

Index 32

Words in **bold** are in the glossary.

WHAT IS THE ARMY?

A big Abrams tank rolls across the land. Army **soldiers** test the tank. They are training. Soldiers always need to be ready to fight.

The United States Army is one branch of the U.S. **military**. It is the largest branch. It has about 1 million members. Its soldiers are trained to fight on land.

JOINING THE ARMY

Men and women can join the Army. They must be 17 to 35 years old. U.S. **citizens** can join. Some noncitizens living lawfully in the U.S. can also join. People who want to join the Army must be healthy and fit.

After joining, soldiers go to basic training. It takes 10 weeks. The new soldiers exercise hard. They run, do push-ups, and more. They learn to use **weapons**. They learn to work together.

After basic training, each soldier has a job. Many fight in land battles. Some are in charge of supplies. Others drive vehicles. Some are doctors and nurses. The U.S. Army has more than 150 kinds of jobs.

Active-duty soldiers serve full-time. Most soldiers in the Army Reserve work part-time. National Guard soldiers work part-time too. Part-time soldiers become active duty if they are needed.

Active-duty soldiers are sent to work at an Army base. A base is like a town just for soldiers. They live on or near the base. Their families can live with them. There are more than 50 Army bases in the United States.

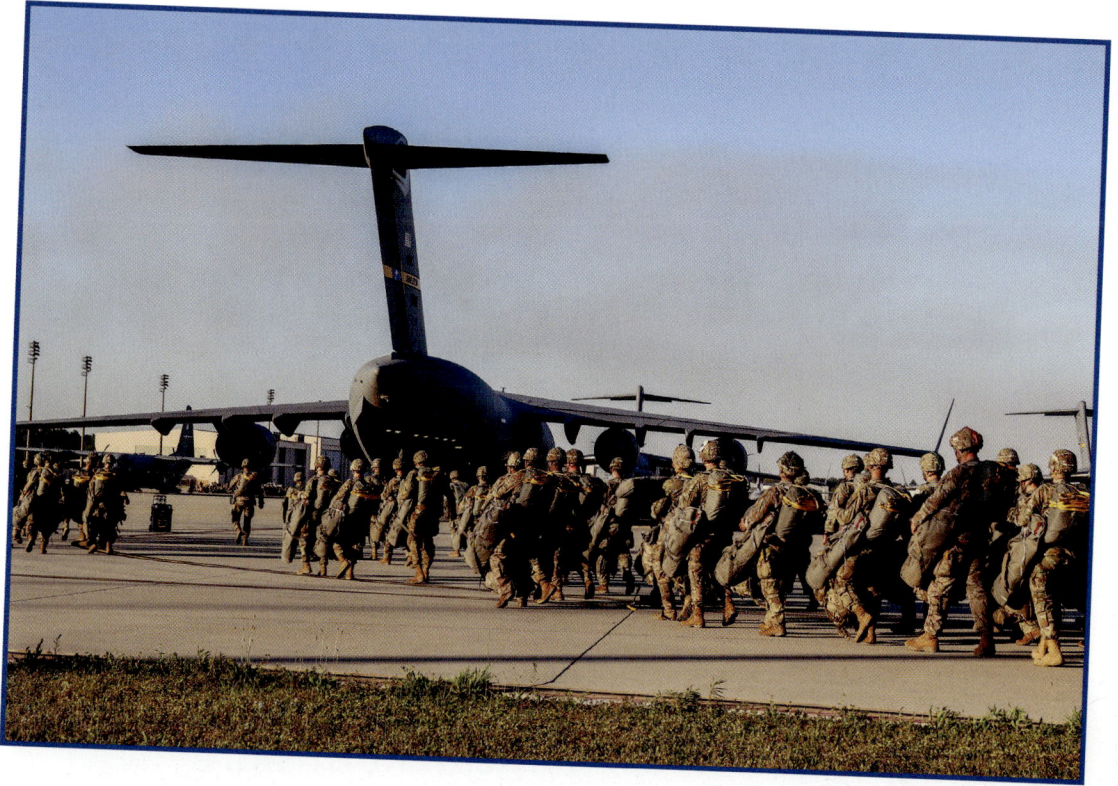

Sometimes soldiers are **deployed**. They might be needed to fight in another country. They might be needed to help after a storm or other natural disaster. Their families stay behind. These **missions** can last for more than a year.

ARMY UNIFORMS AND GEAR

People in the Army wear uniforms. They often wear Army Combat Uniforms (ACUs) to work on bases. They also wear these uniforms when they are in battle. Some uniforms are worn for parades and special events.

The ACU is made in **camouflage**. This helps soldiers blend into their surroundings. It makes them harder to see. This keeps them safer when fighting enemies.

service uniforms

Army Combat Uniforms

Soldiers have different kinds of gear. Some gear helps keep them safe. A helmet can protect the head. Soldiers might wear bulletproof vests. These vests provide protection from bullets.

Soldiers might use systems to find **targets**. One lets them see targets from more than 3 miles (5 kilometers) away. It works at night and in fog or smoke.

Some soldiers work in places with hot weather. They ride in tanks and other vehicles. It can become very hot inside. They can wear vests filled with cold water. A vest is worn against the body under the uniform. Vests help keep soldiers cool.

Soldiers might need to drop into enemy land from the air. They jump out of planes. They use parachutes to land safely.

ARMY VEHICLES AND WEAPONS

The Army has many machines and vehicles. Some move soldiers or carry supplies. Some are for battles.

The Humvee does many jobs. It carries soldiers, guns, and **missiles**. It can be used as an **ambulance** for hurt soldiers. Thick metal covers its sides. This helps protect the people inside.

Humvee

The Apache is an attack helicopter. It is small and fast. It fires **rockets** and missiles. The missiles can attack enemy aircraft. The rockets can hit ground targets. The Apache can track 128 targets at once.

Apaches

Chinook

Other helicopters move people and supplies. The Chinook is a heavy-lift helicopter. It uses a hook to lift and move tanks and other vehicles. It can also be loaded with supplies. The Chinook can carry more than 30 people.

The Abrams is a huge fighting tank. It weighs as much as nine elephants! The top part of the tank holds a powerful main gun. It also has two machine guns. The tank's tracks help it move easily over rough ground.

Abrams tank

Bradley

The Bradley looks like a tank.
But it is smaller and not as heavy.
The Bradley moves quickly. It carries
soldiers into battle. The Bradley
has two guns. It can also carry a
missile system.

Most soldiers who fight carry the M4 rifle. It weighs about 7 pounds (3 kilograms). At this light weight, it's easy to carry. It can be fired fast. It shoots up to 950 bullets per minute.

Soldiers shoot some weapons from far away. The MK19 is heavy. Soldiers fire it from the ground. It can hit targets more than 1 mile (1.6 km) away.

LIFE IN THE ARMY

The daily lives of soldiers are different depending on their jobs. Those who live on bases often start each day with exercise. Then they go to their jobs. They have free time in the evenings and on the weekends.

Soldiers must always be ready to fight. They practice with their weapons. They take classes to learn new skills. They train with their teams.

The Army does more than fight. Its doctors and nurses help in countries where there is sickness. Soldiers clean up and rebuild towns after storms.

Soldiers helped clean up after a hurricane hit Puerto Rico in 2017.

Soldiers stay in the Army between two and six years. Some join again. They make the Army their **career**.

The men and women of the U.S. Army are brave. They work hard to keep the United States safe.

GLOSSARY

ambulance (AM-byuh-luhnts)—a vehicle that takes sick or injured people to a hospital

camouflage (KA-muh-flahzh)—coloring or covering that makes animals, people, and objects look like their surroundings

career (kuh-REER)—the type of work a person does, usually over many years

citizen (SI-tuh-zuhn)—a member of a country or state who has the right to live there

deploy (di-PLOY)—to move troops into position for military action

military (MIL-uh-ter-ee)—the armed forces of a country

missile (MISS-uhl)—an explosive weapon that is thrown or shot at a distant target

mission (MISH-uhn)—a military task

rocket (ROK-it)—a weapon that flies through the air and moves by pushing fuel from one end

soldier (SOLE-jur)—a person who is in an army

target (TAR-git)—an object at which to aim or shoot

weapon (WEP-uhn)—something used for fighting

READ MORE

Kirkman, M. *The Truth About Life as a U.S. Army Soldier*. North Mankato, MN: Capstone Press, 2020.

Kohl, Peter. *My Dad Is in the Army*. New York: PowerKids Press, 2016.

Marx, Mandy R. *Amazing U.S. Army Facts*. North Mankato, MN: Capstone Press, 2017.

INTERNET SITES

Ducksters: US Government: United States Armed Forces
www.ducksters.com/history/us_government/united_states_armed_forces.php

Kiddle: United States Army Facts for Kids
kids.kiddle.co/United_States_Army

U.S. Army: About the Army: Tanks and Fighting Vehicles
www.goarmy.com/about/army-vehicles-and-equipment/tanks-and-fighting-vehicles.html

INDEX

ambulances, 18
Army Reserve, 9

bases, 10, 12, 26
basic training, 7, 8
Bradleys, 23
bulletproof vests, 14

camouflage, 12

deployment, 11
disasters, 11
doctors, 8, 28

exercising, 7, 26

helicopters, 20–21
    Apaches, 20
    Chinooks, 21
helmets, 14
Humvees, 18

joining, 6–7, 29

M4 rifles, 24
missiles, 18, 20, 23
MK19s, 25

National Guard, 9
nurses, 8, 28

parachutes, 16

rockets, 20

storms, 11, 28
supplies, 8, 18, 21

tanks, 4, 16, 21, 22, 23
targeting systems, 15
targets, 15, 20, 25

uniforms, 12

vests, 14, 16